W9-CKH-984

# Going Along With
# LEWIS &
# CLARK

## by Barbara Fifer

**MONTANA**
M A G A Z I N E

For Uncle Wade, who told me stories, and the next generation of explorers: Brandon, Brandt, Clayton, Deion, Erin, Garrett, Greggory, and Savannah.

## About place names

From the fall of 1803 until the fall of 1806, the Lewis and Clark Expedition traveled through areas that were not states or territories yet. For ease in reading, we have used current place names. Readers should imagine the words "present day" before every state or city name west of St. Louis.

ISBN 1-56037-219-2

© 2000 American & World Geographic Publishing/Montana Magazine

This book may not be reproduced in whole or in part by any means (with the exception of short quotes for the purpose of review) without the permission of the publisher.

For more information on our books write:
Farcountry Press
P.O. Box 5630
Helena, MT 59604
call: (800) 654-1105
or visit our online bookshop at
www.montanamagazine.com

Printed in Korea

# Illustration credits

front cover: watercolors and sketch by Bob Everton; Lewis and Clark from Edgar S. Paxson mural, "Lewis and Clark at the Three Forks," Montana State Capitol, transparency courtesy Montana Historical Society. (See more information below.) Background photo by Roland Reed, reproduced courtesy of Kramer Gallery, Minneapolis. These tipis are Blackfeet, of a later time. The Corps saw many Plains Indian tipis, and even traveled with one, but they never visited a Blackfeet camp.

back cover: Entire mural by Edgar S. Paxson (1852-1919), "Lewis and Clark at the Three Forks." The artist shows Meriwether Lewis wearing a tri-cornered officer's hat, the type worn during the Revolutionary War. Since Paxson's day, historians have rediscovered that the War Department designed new army uniforms during the 1790s and early 1800s. The type of hat that captains Lewis and Clark would have been issued is shown in a photograph at the top of page 11. But whether the captains wore their uniform hats on that nice July Thursday in 1805 when they reached the Three Forks, no one knows.

page 3: photo by Fred Pflughoft

pages 4-5: Lewis portrait and Clark portrait courtesy Independence National Historic Park, Philadelphia; elkskin journal and writing desk photos by J. Agee; watercolor and map by Bob Everton

pages 6-7: sketches from The Journals of Patrick Gass, Member of the Lewis and Clark Expedition (1807; repr. 1997, Mountain Press)

pages 8-9: "York in the Mandan Lodge," by Charles M. Russell, courtesy Montana Historical Society; photo by J. Agee

pages 10-11: sketch by Bob Everton; photos by J. Agee

pages 12-13: watercolor and sketches by Bob Everton; photos by J. Agee

pages 14-15: map by Bob Smith; photo by J. Agee

pages 16-17: photos by Larry Mayer; map by Bob Everton

pages 18-19: sketch by Bob Everton; Highwood Mountains photo by Rick Graetz; confluence of Missouri and Marias rivers photo by Chuck Haney; Great Falls photo courtesy Montana Historical Society Photo Archives

pages 20-21: mountain range photo by Douglass Dye; Sacajawea fountain photo by J. Agee; Ecola State Park photo by James Blank

pages 22-23: watercolors and sketch by Bob Everton

pages 24-25: watercolor and sketch by Bob Everton; photos courtesy Montana Historical Society Photo Archives

pages 26-27: sketch from The Journals of Patrick Gass, Member of the Lewis and Clark Expedition; spyglass photo by J. Agee; Indians photo courtesy Montana Historical Society Photo Archives; Fort Leavenworth photo by James Blank

pages 28-29: Missouri River photo by James Blank; Charles M. Russell painting, "Lewis and Clark Meeting Indians at Ross's Hole," Montana State Capitol, John Smart/John Reddy photo courtesy Montana Historical Society; beads photo by J. Agee

pages 30-31: photo courtesy Montana Historical Society Photo Archives; peace pipe sketch by Bob Everton; Blackfeet sketch courtesy Montana Historical Society Photo Archives; trade goods photo by J. Agee

pages 32-33: watercolors by Bob Everton; goat photo by Mike Anich; prairie dog photo by Terry McCormac

pages 34-35: black and white photos courtesy Montana Historical Society Photo Archives; color photo by James Blank; watercolors by Bob Everton

pages 36-37: watercolors by Bob Everton; photo by Chuck Haney

pages 38-39: color photo by J. Agee; black and white photo from Olin D. Wheeler, The Trail of Lewis and Clark (1905); watercolors by Bob Everton

pages 40-41: watercolor by Bob Everton; Lolo Hot Springs sketch by John Mix Stanley

pages 42-43: sketch by Bob Everton; photos by J. Agee

pages 44-45: color photo by J. Agee; watercolor by Bob Everton; black and white photo courtesy Montana Historical Society Photo Archives

pages 46-47: photo by Rick Graetz; J. K. Ralston painting, "Clark on the Yellowstone" hangs in First Interstate Bank, Livingston, MT, transparency courtesy J. Agee

page 48: photo by Fred Pflughoft

Book design by Bob Smith

# Contents

*"End of the Trail" statue, Seaside, Oregon where the salt-making camp was*

## Meriwether Lewis

Lewis was President Thomas Jefferson's secretary when Jefferson asked him to lead this expedition. Lewis was an army captain. He asked a friend from the army, William Clark, to help him lead the Corps of Discovery. (That's what the men started calling themselves once they were on their way. It is pronounced CORE, and means a group of people.)

Lewis and Clark wrote in their journals about what they and their men saw and did. The sergeants had to keep journals also, but some of those are lost. When we read these journals today, sometimes it is like being right beside them—and sometimes they do not tell us enough!

## The Expedition's Mission

Thomas Jefferson was a scientist as well as President of the United States. In 1803, he sent Americans to France to buy the Louisiana Territory. France had claimed the land, given it to Spain, and taken it back again. Jefferson wanted the land for future U.S. settlement, but he also thought scientists should learn about the region and what it held. He sent the Corps of Discovery to find out.

He told Lewis to draw maps, keep track of the weather, write down vocabularies and beliefs of Indian nations, collect plants and animals, watch for natural resources, and make notes on rivers and good farming land.

This is a reproduction of the only surviving notebook carried on the expedition, which was William Clark's and has an elkskin cover. Today the original is at the Missouri Historical Society in St. Louis. When the captains got home and wrote final versions of their journals, they must have thrown away the original notebooks.

## Seaman

Lewis took along his Newfoundland retriever, Seaman, who helped hunt and guard. These big dogs weigh 110 to 150 pounds, and have thick hair for warmth, and webbed feet for swimming. One evening, Lewis and Seaman were walking on the banks of the Missouri river when a buffalo calf joined them. The little calf seemed curious. But he was also afraid of the big dog, and stayed close to Lewis's side—the side away from Seaman!

# captains

## Louisiana Territory

The Louisiana Purchase nearly doubled the size of the United States.

Today's state of Louisiana was only a small part of the Louisiana Territory.

The purchase included most of the land between the Mississippi River and the Rocky Mountains, except Texas and eastern New Mexico.

LOUISIANA PURCHASE

## Espontoon

Lewis carried an espontoon (*es-PAHN-toon*), which was like a spear, but with an open-work top. About six feet long, Lewis's espontoon was as tall as he was. He could use it as a hiking stick, or to steady the very long barrel of his rifle.

Once, when Lewis was all alone and his gun was unloaded, a grizzly bear chased him. There was no time to load the gun, so he ran into the nearby Missouri River. Then Lewis turned and faced the bear, with only the espontoon to defend himself. Luckily, the bear decided to walk away, leaving Lewis wet but unharmed.

## The United States in 1803

- included 17 states, and no more would join until 1820

- had declared independence 27 years earlier

- had adopted the Constitution 14 years earlier

*Clark's field desk would have looked like this. Gentlemen carried them when they traveled. Clark's was broken in September 1805, when the horse carrying it fell down a mountain side. Joseph Field hewed a slab of wood as a lap desk and gave it to Clark for Christmas at Fort Clatsop.*

## William Clark

Clark had been an army captain, and at one time was Lewis's commander. The army insisted that he had to be a lieutenant for the expedition—lower than Captain Lewis. Lewis argued against this, but lost. Then, Lewis decided they would tell everyone Clark was also a captain. The two called each other "co-captain" and always acted as equals.

Clark had red hair. Shoshone (show-SHOW-knee) chief Cameahwait (come-MAY-uh-wait) had never seen red hair before. He tied seashells in Clark's hair to decorate it in Shoshone style.

# Who they were...

**Enlisted men in the permanent party**

**1st Squad**
Sergeant Nathaniel Pryor
John Collins
Pierre Cruzatte
George Gibson
Hugh Hall
Thomas Howard
Francois Labiche
George Shannon
John Shields
Peter M. Weiser
Joseph Whitehouse

**2nd Squad**
Sergeant Charles Floyd
Joseph Field
Reubin Field
Robert Frazer
Patrick Gass
(elected sergeant to replace Floyd)
Hugh McNeal
John B. Thompson
Richard Windsor

**3rd Squad**
Sergeant John Ordway
William Bratton
John Colter
Silas Goodrich
John Potts
William Werner
Alexander Willard

## Return party
(EXPLAINED ON PAGE 22)
Cpl. Richard Warfington
John Dame
John Boley
John Robertson (or Robinson)
Ebenezer Tuttle
Isaac White
John Newman
(expelled for mutinous talk in 1804)
Moses B. Reed
(expelled for desertion in 1804)

# The Enlisted Men

Thomas Jefferson told Captain Lewis to choose sturdy frontiersmen who knew how to live off the land. He warned Lewis not to take "young gentlemen."

French,
English,
Omaha,
Hidatsa,
Plains Sign,
Mandan

Languages the enlisted men knew included English, French, Omaha, Hidatsa, Mandan, and Plains Indian sign language.

And so, the Corps of Discovery met many Indian nations whose language were new to the men.

*Patrick Gass, late in his life. He lived to be 100, and was the last survivor of the Corps.*

John Boley, who was in the return party from Fort Mandan to St. Louis in spring 1805, joined the Zebulon Pike expedition the following year. On that trip, Pikes Peak in Colorado was seen at a distance and named.

## Some members

of the expedition fell in love with the Rocky Mountains. After the expedition ended in 1806, at least seven men returned there, some for the rest of their lives.

John Colter was first—even before the expedition ended! In North Dakota on the return trip, he asked for an early discharge from the army. He wanted to join trappers heading upriver. The captains checked to see if the other men agreed, and asked them to promise no one else would leave early. The men approved, and several gave Colter useful presents.

The year after returning home, Sergeant Patrick Gass was the first to publish an expedition journal. Here's how an artist for Gass's book imagined the men building one of the winter forts—with the men working in their dress uniforms!

## Communication

None of the men could speak the Sioux language.

Privates Cruzatte and Labiche had French fathers and Omaha mothers, and they spoke both those languages, in addition to English.

During the Corps' tense visit with the Teton Sioux (TEE-tahn SUE), Cruzatte talked to some Omaha captives. They said the Sioux were thinking about killing the Corps, so Labiche warned the captains. Extra guards were assigned to the boats, and nothing happened.

## Special skills

MEN AT WORK

Everyone needed to be a hunter and a woodsman, but some enlisted men had additional skills that were very important.

Labiche was an excellent boatman and experienced Indian trader.

Cruzatte knew the Missouri River—and its native peoples—as far as the Mandan villages.

Willard, Shields, and Bratton were blacksmiths. They could fix the metal tools, and even make useful gadgets.

Shields was also a gunsmith, and sometimes fixed guns others thought couldn't be repaired.

Gass and Shields were carpenters.

Cruzatte and Gibson could play the violin, or "fiddle," as the men called it.

At Fort Mandan, the blacksmiths made useful tools from a broken metal stove, and traded them for corn. They made battleaxes, arrowheads, and hide scrapers.

**YOUNGEST**
George Shannon was the youngest enlisted man, turning 19 during 1804.

**OLDEST**
John Shields was the oldest enlisted man, at 35.

**COUSINS**
Charles Floyd and Nathaniel Pryor were cousins.

**BROTHERS**
Reubin and Joseph Field were brothers.

**LEWIS**
Lewis was 30 that year

**CLARK**
Clark was 34.

During the first winter, the captains watched the men at work and play. Which ones had the needed skills to go all the way to the Pacific? The journals included lists like this, with misspelled names, but we don't know what the symbols mean.

# Who they were...

## York

York, an African American slave, had been raised with William Clark, who freed him a few years after the trip. Clark called him "my servant" in the journals.

York was a big man and a good hunter. He shared all the duties of the Corps. Before Sacagawea joined the expedition, York sometimes collected wild greens for meals. The men liked the change in their diet of meat, meat, meat.

Some Indian people thought York's dark skin color came from paint. York allowed them to try to rub off the "paint." Then he showed them that his scalp—where you wouldn't put paint—was the same color.

During the expedition, York carried his own rifle and hunted for food. At that time, it was illegal in slave-holding states for a slave even to use a gun. York went out hunting alone as well as with other men, and was ready to help if there was an attack.

After 1811, Clark finally freed York, who set up his own freighting business with a horse-drawn wagon.

## The Civilians

In addition to the soldiers, a few civilians were hired, as boatmen, interpreters, and river guides. Clark took his servant, York, along.

Although no picture of York exists, artist Charles M. Russell imagined this scene in a Mandan lodge during the winter of 1804-1805. From the journals, it seems that York didn't mind when Indian people were so amazed at his dark skin. He was a big man, but a good dancer, which also surprised them.

## George Drouillard

George Drouillard (DREW-yer) was a good hunter and an experienced boatman on the Missouri River. He was the most consistently useful civilian the captains hired. His knowledge of the river was very helpful to the Corps of Discovery.

Both captains often took him along when exploring ahead of the main party. Drouillard spoke the Shawnee language of his mother, French learned from his French-Canadian father, and also knew Plains Indian sign language.

## French boatmen

Several French boatmen, led by Baptist Deschamps, were hired to help during the first summer. They manned the red pirogue (per-ROAG, a flat-bottomed canoe), and shared their knowledge of the Missouri River. At least some of them spent the winter at Fort Mandan and returned to St. Louis in the spring of 1805.

# Sacagawea

Sacagawea (*suh-KAH-guh-wee-uh*), a Shoshone from the Rocky Mountains, was about 17 years old in 1804. She was Charbonneau's wife. When she was about 12 years old, she and other Shoshones had been captured by the Hidatsa near the Missouri River's headwaters and taken to North Dakota. She spoke Shoshone and Hidatsa.

She was hired as an interpreter, not a guide. Three times she recognized places in southwestern Montana that she remembered from childhood. Those were the only times she helped point the way.

Her job was to translate from the Shoshone language. Most importantly, she helped the Corps buy horses from the Shoshone and get other help in crossing the Rockies.

Many of the Indians the Corps met never allowed women to go on war parties. So, when these Indians discovered the Corps, and saw a woman and a baby in it, they decided the strangers were friendly. Sacagawea also helped the Corps by gathering food and medicinal plants.

An important contribution came when she kept a cool head during a canoe accident that her husband caused. As the boat filled with water and he yelled in fear, she grabbed items about to float away. These included medicines and some of the captain's journals and maps.

# "Pompy"

Jean Baptiste Charbonneau (*SHAR-bon-no*) was born February 11, 1805, and was 55 days old when the expedition set out from Fort Mandan. He rode in a cradleboard on his mother Sacagawea's back.

Clark was fond of the little boy, and nicknamed him "Pompy." Clark asked his parents to let Pompy come to St. Louis to attend school. They sent the boy to Clark when he was about 6 years old. When he was 18, a visiting German prince for whom his father had translated took him to Europe. He spent six years there.

After returning to the U.S., he worked as a mountain man and guide in the west.

# Charbonneau

Toussaint (*TWO-sahnt*) Charbonneau was hired at Fort Mandan as an interpreter. He spoke French and Hidatsa, but not English at first. He had two Shoshone wives, but only the younger one, Sacagawea, decided to go along on the trip.

He was not too good at anything besides cooking, but that was an important skill.

# Everyone votes

Choosing a location to spend the winter of 1805-1806 was difficult. Some wanted to stay near the Pacific coast, and some wanted to go back up the Columbia River. Others thought they should explore along the coast.

The captains decided to settle the question by allowing everyone to vote. Everyone—including York and Sacagawea, who both couldn't vote in the United States at that time—gave an opinion.

Clark wrote that "Janey" voted for any place with plenty of roots to eat. This was the nickname he'd given to Sacagawea.

Staying near, but not on, the coast won the election.

*No one knows what Sacagawea and baby Jean Baptiste looked like, but many statues and the U.S. one-dollar coin honor her. This statue is on the North Dakota Capitol grounds in Bismarck. In North Dakota, her name is spelled Sakakawea because of how the Hidatsa people pronounced it.*

## Interpreting

It was slow and difficult to communicate, since many different languages were being used. When trying to buy Shoshone horses to carry baggage over the mountains, Lewis, in English, told Drouillard what to say.

Drouillard, in French, told Charbonneau.

Charbonneau, in Hidatsa, told Sacagawea.

Sacagawea, in Shoshone, told Cameahwait.

After Cameahwait answered, the translation had to go back around before Lewis had the chief's answer.

# What they wore...

## The men had army uniforms

of the day, and the captains' uniforms included swords and brass buttons. When they left St. Louis in 1804, their uniforms would have looked bright and fresh like the reproductions pictured here.

**GARAGE SALE**

## Leather Clothing

By mid–May 1805, the Corps' summer clothing was wearing out and they began making leather pants and moccasins. They used deer and elk hides. In another six weeks, everyone was in leather clothing.

During the winter of 1805–1806 at Fort Clatsop, their wool clothing wore out also.

Near Little Sioux, Iowa, on the homeward trip, the Corps met fur traders heading upriver. Some of the men eagerly traded their deerskin shirts and beaver hats for linen shirts and cloth hats.

## First time in a backpack

When he went ahead up the Missouri looking for the Great Falls in 1805, Captain Lewis wore a knapsack. He used a blanket to make it, probably copying an idea from Indians he had seen. With a smile he wrote that it was the first time he had used such a thing, "and I am fully convinced that it will not be the last."

◀ The leather clothes may have looked like this. The moccasins would not have been decorated unless the men bought them from Indian women.

This is a reproduction of an officer's dress uniform like the captains wore.

Enlisted men's dress hat were like top hats, but not as tall, and had a piece of fur for decoration. Their uniforms were plainer than officers' clothes.

# Elves wanted!

Indians around Fort Clatsop didn't wear moccasins, so the Corps had to make their own instead of trading for them. The men didn't like tanning hides and sewing clothing. But they needed shoes for the homeward trip. By the end of winter, they had made clothing and about 10 pairs of moccasins apiece, just enough to get them to St. Louis.

The Corps also took presents and trade goods for Indians. These are described on pages 28-29.

This deer hide is cut out for a moccasin, ready to be sewn together. Each man had to make many pairs for himself during the trip, after his army boots wore out.

# Moccasins

Clark mentioned men of the Corps wearing moccasins in September 1804, even before they wintered with the Mandan-Hidatsa.

That winter, Clark learned two interesting phrases from the Mandan. He was trying to make peace between the Mandan and the Arikara (uh-RICK-uh-ruh). One of the Mandan chiefs said he would like to "take off his moccasins at night." This meant to be at peace, not staying on guard.

Clark also wrote that a Mandan leader said some Arikara villages were "making their moccasins." This meant gathering supplies to go to war.

Moccasins for winter could be made of heavy buffalo hide, as the Mandans did. Thinner deer or elk hide was used for summer. When the ground was very stony, the men sewed additional layers of hide to their moccasins' soles.

Clark found another use for moccasins during his homeward trip on the Yellowstone River. He had moccasins put on the horses, too, and wrote that this helped them walk on the rocky ground.

# Things they took...

## Tomahawks

These tools were invented by Native Americans and adopted by white immigrants. They could be used as a weapon, but more often served other purposes. The iron tomahawk issued by the army was an ax-and-hammer combination, about 18 inches long. Some tomahawks even had built-in peace pipes.

They were an important, all-purpose tool that the men used constantly.

The Corps used their tomahawks to make many dugout canoes. They butchered bison, deer, elk, and other game with them.

When the men had to portage around the Great Falls of the Missouri, Clark surveyed the best route for them to walk. Then he pounded stakes into the ground with a tomahawk to mark the way.

When the men made wagons for the portage, they used tomahawks to cut and to pound.

The Corps' three winter camps were built with the help of tomahawks.

## Knives, tomahawks, and rifles

issued to the men came from the U.S. arsenal in Harpers Ferry, Virginia. John Shields could repair guns and tools, but there was no way to replace a lost one. Many times the journals mention that one of the men had left his tomahawk or knife behind. He had to walk back to last night's campsite, find the precious tool, then catch up with the expedition. And they didn't stop to wait for him.

*Fifteen men of the Corps carried the first U.S. army regulation rifle, which was brand new. The barrel alone was 33 inches long. It was a flintlock, which meant the bullet was pushed down the barrel. Preparing the gunpowder and loading the gun took at least 30 seconds. During that time, a grizzly bear could run more than 800 feet on flat ground!*

*Other men, including the captains and York, preferred their own "Kentucky" rifles. These were also flintlocks, but had an even longer barrel.*

*The men made their round bullets by melting lead, and pouring it into molds. Gunpowder to fire the bullets had to be kept dry. But they were splashing around in rivers all day! So, the powder was stored in airtight cans made of lead. (Each had four pounds of powder placed inside eight pounds of lead.) When a can was opened, its powder was shared among the men. Each man had to keep his own powder dry. Then the lead can was melted and made into bullets.*

# Navigating and mapping

Clark was a surveyor, and before the trip Lewis learned to navigate by the stars from a Philadelphia scientist. They used special tools to locate positions by looking at stars and planets. Their method was very simple by today's standards, but the maps Clark drew gave the world the best picture yet of the land and waters between the Missouri and the Pacific. He spent weeks at both winter forts drawing. In St. Louis after the trip, Clark finished the maps over two years.

*Sextant*

Some tools they used for navigating and mapmaking were:

**chronometer**—an extremely accurate type of clock, and a new invention then.

**sextant**—used to locate position according to stars and planets. This instrument was only 50 years old. First Lewis or Clark used the sextant to measure between the horizon and two different stars or planets. Then he plugged the measurements into a standard math equation. By looking up the answer on a chart, he found longitude and latitude. Longitude is the measurement of east to west, and latitude is north to south.

**quadrant**—simpler ancestor of the sextant, used by explorers such as Columbus.

**spyglass**—a small telescope.

**dry-card mariners' compass**—with a needle that floated over the "card" that showed north/east/south/west, rather than floating in liquid. Clark's compass today is in the Smithsonian Institution in Washington, D.C.

*Clark's compass*

*Blowing this boatman's horn made a loud, harsh blast. It sounded like the airhorns that today's boaters and sports fans use. The main party used it to give their location to men who had gone out alone to hunt or scout ahead.*

*A plant or leaf press you could buy today wouldn't be very different from the one Captain Lewis used. This is a reproduction of his.*

## Candles

The last of the Corps' candles were used up in January at Fort Clatsop. No worry—candlemolds and wicks were in the baggage. New candles were made with elk tallow.

# Where they went...

## The Corps was to follow

the Missouri River all the way to its headwaters in the Rocky Mountains. Then they were to find a good way to cross the mountains and go down streams leading to the Columbia River. After that, they would float down the Columbia to the Pacific Ocean.

They had information and maps from recent explorers, and from traders in St. Louis, to help part of the way. John Evans had gone up the Missouri to the Mandan-Hidatsa villages in North Dakota only seven years before Lewis talked to him in St. Louis during autumn 1803. A little over ten years before the Corps set out, Robert Gray, an American, had sailed into the mouth of the Columbia River from the Pacific. The captains studied maps that Evans and Gray had drawn.

But over the 1,400 miles in between, they would have to find their own way, and ask Native Americans they met. As they learned new things, they changed their travel plans. For example, Jefferson and Lewis thought some of the men would catch a trading ship on the Pacific Ocean in the fall of 1805. Going home by sea, they'd take journals, maps, and animal specimens. The Corps reached the Pacific after trading ships were gone for the year. But even before that, the captains had decided they needed every man to help on the homeward trip.

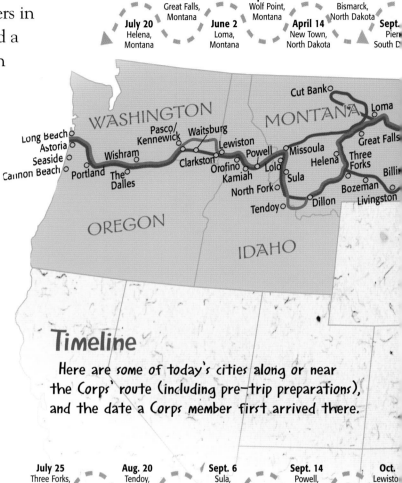

### 1805

| | | |
|---|---|---|
| **June 13** Great Falls, Montana | **April 30** Wolf Point, Montana | **Oct. 19** Bismarck, North Dakota |
| **July 20** Helena, Montana | **June 2** Loma, Montana | **April 14** New Town, North Dakota | **Sept.** Pier South D |

## Timeline

Here are some of today's cities along or near the Corps' route (including pre-trip preparations), and the date a Corps member first arrived there.

| | | | | |
|---|---|---|---|---|
| **July 25** Three Forks, Montana | **Aug. 20** Tendoy, Idaho | **Sept. 6** Sula, Montana | **Sept. 14** Powell, Idaho | **Oct.** Lewisto Clarkst WA |
| **Aug. 9** Dillon, Montana | **Aug. 21** North Fork, Idaho | **Sept. 13** Lolo, Montana | **Sept. 26** Orofino, Idaho | |

### 1805

*This is a model of Columbia Rediviva, the ship that Robert Gray sailed into the mouth of the Columbia River in 1792. His maps of the far western end of their own trip helped the Corps.*

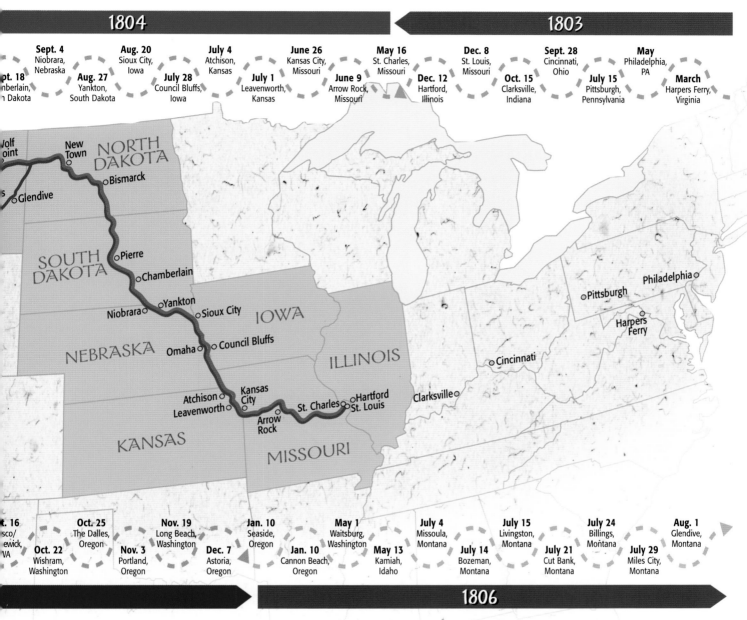

Westward to the Pacific Ocean
Return trip to St. Louis

**1804**

| Sept. 4 Niobrara, Nebraska | Aug. 20 Sioux City, Iowa | July 4 Atchison, Kansas | June 26 Kansas City, Missouri | May 16 St. Charles, Missouri |
| Aug. 27 Yankton, South Dakota | July 28 Council Bluffs, Iowa | July 1 Leavenworth, Kansas | June 9 Arrow Rock, Missouri | |

pt. 18 ...berlain, ...h Dakota

**1803**

| Dec. 8 St. Louis, Missouri | Sept. 28 Cincinnati, Ohio | May Philadelphia, PA |
| Dec. 12 Hartford, Illinois | Oct. 15 Clarksville, Indiana | July 15 Pittsburgh, Pennsylvania | March Harpers Ferry, Virginia |

Wolf Point · New Town · NORTH DAKOTA · Bismarck · Glendive · SOUTH DAKOTA · Pierre · Chamberlain · Yankton · Niobrara · Sioux City · IOWA · NEBRASKA · Omaha · Council Bluffs · ILLINOIS · Atchison · Kansas City · Leavenworth · Arrow Rock · St. Charles · Hartford · St. Louis · Clarksville · KANSAS · MISSOURI · Pittsburgh · Philadelphia · Harpers Ferry · Cincinnati

| t. 16 sco/ ewick, VA | Oct. 25 The Dalles, Oregon | Nov. 19 Long Beach, Washington | Jan. 10 Seaside, Oregon | May 1 Waitsburg, Washington | July 4 Missoula, Montana | July 15 Livingston, Montana | July 24 Billings, Montana | Aug. 1 Glendive, Montana |
| Oct. 22 Wishram, Washington | Nov. 3 Portland, Oregon | Dec. 7 Astoria, Oregon | Jan. 10 Cannon Beach, Oregon | May 13 Kamiah, Idaho | July 14 Bozeman, Montana | July 21 Cut Bank, Montana | July 29 Miles City, Montana | |

**1806**

# Hopping from "state" to "state"

Leaving St. Louis in May 1804, the Corps followed the Missouri River upstream roughly west across today's state of Missouri. At Kansas City, the river's bend led them generally northwest until they reached the Mandan-Hidatsa villages near Bismarck, North Dakota.

Through part of the Great Plains, the Missouri River today forms state borders. Traveling the river in 1804, the Corps stopped to eat or rest or camp for the night wherever they saw a good spot to land. In modern terms, this could mean lunch in Kansas and camp in Missouri, or camp in Nebraska and stopping to visit Indians in Iowa.

The Missouri forms only a small part of South Dakota's border (with Nebraska). After that, their trail passed through only one state at a time, by today's map—until they came to the Columbia River. This is today's border between Washington and Oregon.

# Finding the way...

**Studying books and maps,** talking with traders and soldiers during the winter at Camp Wood, the captains learned as much as they could about the land ahead. At Fort Mandan, they quizzed Indian and white visitors.

But no one had visited all the land between Fort Mandan and the mouth of the Columbia River. They were in for some surprises and some puzzles. Sometimes the whole Corps of Discovery got lost. Sometimes one or a few men were sent out to hunt or explore and had trouble finding their way back. Usually, they just camped alone for a night or two while looking for the big group.

**HELP WANTED**

*Pompeys Pillar, near Billings, Montana, is a 200-foot-tall sandstone rock. Captain Clark named it for Sacagawea's son, whom he called "Pomp" or "Pompey." Clark carved and painted his name and the date on trees, but what he carved here is the only physical sign left of the expedition.*

## Past the last white settlement

After leaving St. Louis, the Corps passed a few white settlements along the Missouri River. The last was near today's Washington, Missouri. But after that they still met white people. A few fur traders and trappers were coming downriver after spending fall and winter working far north and west. Everyone would pull to shore for a visit. The captains asked for information about places ahead of them, and even traded some goods.

Indians of other tribes, and white traders from Canada, visited the Mandan-Hidatsa villages that winter of 1804-1805, and also were quizzed about places they knew.

After the Corps left the Mandan-Hidatsa villages in spring 1805, they did not meet any more whites for nearly 19 months.

**ROAD ENDS**

## Continental Divide

The Continental Divide follows the highest points in the Rocky Mountains. From it, water on the east flows to the Missouri/Mississippi river system and to the Atlantic Ocean. Water on the west side flows to the Pacific.

When Lewis arrived on the divide in August 1805, he was scouting ahead of the main party with Sergeant Gass and interpreters Charbonneau and Drouillard. Standing on Lemhi Pass, he saw many mountain ranges ahead—and they still had some snow on top!

The Rockies were not like the familiar Appalachians of the east. Mount Mitchell, in North Carolina, stands 6,684 feet above sea level, and is the highest mountain in the eastern United States. On Lemhi Pass, Lewis's men stood at 7,372 feet. Some mountains nearby rose above 10,000 feet.

## Rocky Mountains

During the winter at Fort Mandan, Hidatsa men who had traveled to or near the Rocky Mountains described them to the captains. Lewis thought they said climbing to the top would take half a day on horseback.

On the other side, they said, a big river flowed to the west through plains. The Salish Indians lived in a large village just over the mountains. No bison roamed these plains, so the Salish lived on large fish caught in that river.

Because they knew that large salmon lived in the Columbia River, the captains thought that the Rockies were a single range of mountains. Unfortunately, the information was incomplete.

Columbia River · Marias R. · Missouri River · Willamette R. · Salmon R. · Yellowstone River · Snake R. · CONTINENTAL DIVIDE · N. Platte R. · S. Platte R. · Platte River · Kansas River · James R. · Big Sioux R. · Missouri River · Mississippi River · PACIFIC OCEAN · ATLANTIC OCEAN · GULF OF MEXICO

## The wrong mountains

Late in May 1805, in central Montana, Captain Clark told Captain Lewis that when he was walking on shore he saw mountains ahead. Lewis then climbed the Missouri River's steep 300-foot bluffs to look. He saw mountains shining with snow, and thought they were the Rockies. He was excited to think the mountains—and the headwaters of the Missouri—were "so near."

But these mountains were the Highwoods, a small isolated range far from the Rockies.

The Corps wouldn't be "so near" to the Rockies for another two and a half months.

*The Highwood Mountains (see story above)*

## The starving teenager

Private George Shannon, still in his teens, was the party's youngest soldier. He was not a very good hunter in the early days of the trip.

One day late in August 1804, the men were in Sioux territory that became South Dakota. Shannon and George Drouillard were sent out to look for the Corps' four horses.

The next day, Drouillard was back. He had walked all night long on the prairie above the Missouri River, but he didn't see the horses—or his partner, Shannon.

The Corps kept moving upriver. On the third day, they met the Yankton Sioux, an important nation to hold a council with. The Corps stopped for two days of visiting.

When they made their campsite, they saw Shannon's footprints. He had passed them and was hurrying ahead, thinking he was still behind! The captains sent Private John Colter ahead to catch Shannon.

On the eighth and tenth days after Shannon had left, the Corps again saw his footprints. Beside them were those of Colter, still following him.

Finally, on the 16th day Shannon was gone, the keelboat crew saw him up ahead. He was sitting on the riverbank, weak and starving, waiting in hopes a trading boat would come along. He thought the Corps was too far ahead for him ever to catch up.

He told the men that he ran out of bullets trying to shoot bison for food. There were plenty of bison. Shannon even carved a wooden bullet, trying to get food. All he had had to eat for more than two weeks were one rabbit and some wild grapes.

That was the longest any of the men ever was lost.

# Decision Point

Lewis and Clark asked many people for information about the Missouri River, but nothing that they had heard made them expect what they found on June 2, 1805, near Loma, Montana. The river seemed to fork! One river flowed from the northwest and one from the southwest, and they were both big.

The only difference was that the one from the north was muddy, just as the Missouri had been across the plains.

The captains were sure the north fork was not the main Missouri. They remembered that the Mandans said the Missouri was clear, not muddy, where it came out of the mountains. Cruzatte, the experienced riverman, and most of the other men were equally sure that they should follow the muddy fork.

*Great Falls of the Missouri*

To decide, Lewis took five men and Clark took six. Lewis's party went up the north river, and Clark's went up the south one. The others camped and dressed skins to make clothing.

When the scouting parties returned in a few days, the captains still thought one thing and the rest disagreed.

So Lewis now took other men and went up the south fork, the one Clark had explored. He went about 10 miles farther than his co-captain had, and found the Great Falls. All of the Corps knew to expect a big waterfall on the Missouri.

Today the area where they camped is still called Decision Point.

*This picture looks down the Missouri River from Decision Point. The Corps was coming upstream when they saw the river ahead was forked. The Missouri, at the top of this picture, was to their left.*

## Not one, but five falls

The Mandan and Hidatsa said the Corps would reach a great waterfall on the Missouri River. It was so big it would take a whole day to portage (walk and carry freight) around.

When Captain Lewis's advance party came to a big falls, he was glad. Then he walked a little farther, to see what the river was like beyond the falls.

But after he passed the falls, he heard another one ahead! So he walked farther, and the same thing happened again. Then, two more times.

The Missouri River's "great falls" was actually a series of five waterfalls within a few miles of each other. Getting around them took a month instead of a day. This delay meant that by the time they got to the Rockies, it was autumn.

## Rows and rows of Rockies

BUMP
AHEAD

The captains expected the Rocky Mountains would be like the Appalachian mountain chain in the east. They expected high but rounded peaks, covered with trees and plants, filled with game. They also thought the Rockies would be one range to go up and over.

But they found that the Rockies were range after range. Almost no game lived in them, and food was scarce.

The Nez Perce people had a trail through the Rockies' Bitterroot Range—but the Corps' Shoshone guide had trouble finding it. By the time the Corps started across the Bitterroots, it was mid-September. The climate and the mountains' height meant that they were already filled with snow.

# Ocean in view?

Traveling down the Columbia River in constant rain, the Corps could hardly wait to reach the Pacific Ocean and rest.

What they didn't know was that the Columbia had a large estuary. An estuary is a long, wide river mouth where ocean waves mix with river water.

On November 7, 1806, the Corps reached the upper end of that estuary, and saw waves breaking on rocky shores. Clark wrote: "Great joy in camp[. W]e are in view of the ocean, this great Pacific Ocean which we have been so long anxious to see."

But the actual ocean coast still was miles away. The estuary's rocks made it hard to find a flat place to camp at night. The wind was cold, and rain fell all the time. While the main group hunkered down at Point Ellice, Washington, privates Colter, Willard, and Shannon tried to go ahead by canoe on November 12. High waves soon sent them back. They reached the coast the following day.

Clark himself didn't reach the ocean until November 18.

# The great waters

On January 6, 1806, Captain Clark was taking some men to the Pacific. They'd heard that a whale had washed up on the beach, and hoped to get some to eat. Sacagawea insisted on going along, since she had not been there yet. Lewis wrote that she said "she had traveled a long way with us to see the great waters, and now that monstrous fish was also to be seen…" With her husband and baby, she went along.

*Pioneer Park in Lewiston, Idaho, has this statue imagining Sacagawea. Perhaps this is how she greeted the "great waters."*

## Rivers have heads and mouths, upstream and downstream

Where a river begins is called its "head" or "headwaters." Where it ends by flowing into a bigger body of water is called its "mouth." "Downstream" means the direction a river flows. Going "upstream" means moving against the water flow.

The Corps of Discovery first went upstream on the Missouri River, the biggest river of the northern Great Plains. They passed the mouths of many smaller rivers, including the Kansas, Platte, Big Sioux, James, Cheyenne, and Yellowstone.

After they crossed the Rockies, the Corps followed the Clearwater River to the Snake River, and on to the Columbia River. The Corps made canoes and followed the Columbia downstream to the Pacific Ocean.

*Ecola State Park, Oregon*

21

# How they traveled...

The first summer (1804), the permanent and the return party traveled together in a keelboat and two pirogues. At Fort Mandan that winter, the men made six dugout canoes.

In the spring, the return party went back to St. Louis in the keelboat.

The permanent party continued up the Missouri in the pirogues and canoes. Lewis wrote that "these little vessels contained every article by which we... expect to subsist or defend ourselves" for 2,000 more miles.

## Keelboating the Missouri

Built in Pittsburgh, Pennsylvania, under Lewis's watchful eye, the keelboat was the Corps' largest vessel. It was 55 feet long and 8 feet wide. Its stern (or back) held a small cabin with a deck on top. The bow (front) held another deck. In the middle was the hold, or cargo area.

During the winter at Camp Wood, the Corps built and installed lockers along the sides. These held cargo and acted as decks. Their lids could be raised for protection during an attack, but this never had to be done.

The men also installed 11 benches. Two men could sit on each bench to row the boat if needed. Removable poles were added to hold awnings over the boat's center and cabin decks.

The boat's keel, or pointed bottom, allowed it to travel upstream, against the river's flow. The keelboat had a mast where two sails could be raised.

Sometimes, when the river was too shallow for rowing, the men had to "pole" the boat forward. Each man in a group would push a long pole against the river bottom, then walk toward the stern, pushing the deck with his feet.

When poling didn't work, because the river was rocky or even more shallow, their last choice was "cordelling" (*core-DELL-ing*). The men walked onshore and pulled the boat with heavy ropes. After their ropes wore out, they had to stop and make more out of twisted animal hides.

The men had to work hard to get the keelboat upriver to the Mandan-Hidatsa villages. As autumn approached, river levels dropped lower and lower. Most of the Missouri River's water came from melted mountain snow, which was gone by that time of year.

Making up the keelboat's crew in 1804 were the captains and some men of the permanent party.

The keelboat carried the return party and a cargo of journals, Clark's first big map, and animal specimens back to St. Louis in the spring of 1805.

*The keelboat had a small cannon on its front (or "bow," pronounced like tree bough) that could be turned in any direction. It was the biggest gun Indians on the Missouri River had seen.*

# The sad story of Experiment

Captain Lewis had a boat frame made of iron at the U.S. armory in Harpers Ferry, Virginia. It weighed 44 pounds, would carry 40 times that weight, and was 36 feet long. Lewis was going to call the boat *Experiment*.

When they got to the upper Missouri River, where water was shallow, the men would put it together. Animal hides would cover the frame. The seams would be waterproofed with sticky pine-tree pitch.

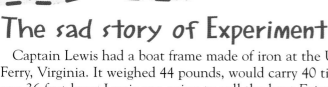

At the Missouri's Great Falls, in Montana, Lewis and Gass, Shields, and Joseph Field worked on the boat. They shot buffalo and elk, then sewed the hides together.

But there were no pine trees here to provide pitch to seal the seams. Lewis mixed beeswax, buffalo fat, and ground-up charcoal to use instead of pitch.

When they first launched *Experiment*, it floated just fine. But, by night, the mixture was falling right off the seams, and the boat leaked.

Lewis wrote in his journal that he was "mortified."

They took the boat apart and buried it in a cache. The white pirogue was too big to float on this shallow part of the river. Now the men had to build two dugout canoes to carry their supplies.

*Making a dugout canoe is simple but hard work. First, chop down a tree. Shape both ends to points. Then start to hollow out the tree with hot coals. Chop away the charred wood with a tomahawk, and smooth out the inside.*

## Pirogues

These flat-bottomed boats could be dugout logs or wooden boats built in a similar shape. Their flat hulls, or bottoms, let them float in very shallow water. They were rowed by men in pairs. The Corps' "red pirogue" (the only name it ever had) had seven oars, and the smaller "white pirogue" had six. Sails could be raised on masts if the wind was right. As much cargo as possible also filled the boats.

Lewis often joked that the white pirogue seemed to have an "evil genie" that "played pranks with her." It was in more accidents and had more problems than the other boats.

**CAUTION
SUNDAY
DRIVERS**

## Canoes of the Columbia River

Near Celilo Falls on the Columbia in fall 1805, the Corps saw a new kind of dugout canoe. It was very wide in the center, and tapered to each end. On the high bow "curious figures" were carved.

To Clark, it was beautiful and "neater made than any I have ever seen." He also saw that its shape allowed it to ride the waves and carry much cargo. The canoe's Indian owner said he had traded a horse to a white man for it downriver. The Corps traded him one of their own canoes, a hatchet, and other trade goods for it.

Getting ready to return upriver on the Columbia in 1806, Captain Lewis sent Drouillard to buy a canoe from the Cathlamet Indians. The Cathlamets valued a boat as much as a wife, Lewis wrote. Drouillard finally had to trade Lewis's uniform dress coat, plus a large amount of tobacco.

## Wagons

To go around the Great Falls of the Missouri, a series of five waterfalls, the men had to walk 18 miles. They built two wagons, designed so that the baggage holders could be removed. When it was time to move the canoes, these rode on the wagons. The wagon wheels were "slices" of cottonwood trees, 22 inches across. The white pirogue's mast was cut in two for axletrees, rods connecting the axles, which the wheels turn on.

The men had to pull these wagons, walking over bumpy, rocky ground that twisted their ankles. Prickly pear cactus covered the ground, and the men's moccasins offered little protection.

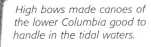

*High bows made canoes of the lower Columbia good to handle in the tidal waters.*

## Horses

When they left Camp Dubois, the Corps had four horses. Along the way to Fort Mandan, they found and lost horses on the prairies. The animals were useful but not required in this country.

Listening to Indian and white visitors during the winter at Fort Mandan, they learned that they needed horses to carry baggage across the Rocky Mountains. They also heard about the Shoshones, who should be east of the Rockies in the fall. These people owned many horses, so the captains intended to buy some.

The Corps did buy from the Shoshones. After crossing the Rockies, they left the horses with Nez Perce people. These excellent horsemen cared for the animals all through the winter of 1805-1806, while the Corps went on to the Pacific.

# Bullboats

*Rowing a bullboat*

When Corps members first saw Mandan and Hidatsa bullboats, they were amazed at how stable the little boats were. They watched two women safely paddle a heavily loaded bullboat across the Missouri River's waves on a windy day. This was the perfect craft for the wide, choppy river!

To build one, people made a bowl-shaped frame of sticks tied together with leather thongs. This was covered with untanned animal hides.

On the 1806 homeward trip, in Montana, Sergeant Pryor and Privates Shannon, Hall, and Windsor were sent from Clark's group with horses to trade for supplies at a British post in Canada. When Indians ran off their horses, the men made two bullboats and headed down the Yellowstone River, then down the Missouri. If they didn't catch up with the Corps, they could still reach St. Louis. They met Clark's group on the Missouri in western North Dakota.

Lewis's group also made some bullboats that summer, to carry baggage and food across the Missouri near the Great Falls.

## On foot

The men often had to walk—on sand, stones, rocks and cactus. On the way to the Mandan–Hidatsa villages, they often had to walk so the boats would float in the shallow Missouri. Sometimes they even had to walk and pull the boats.

At the Great Falls of the Missouri, they walked around the falls, pulling wagons that held their canoes and baggage.

On the Columbia River in 1805, even though they were floating downstream, they often had to portage around rapids. They carried boats and supplies on their backs.

*Women making a bullboat frame*

# People they met...

<table>
<tr><td>

## Some Indian tribes the Corps visited

Kickapoo
Osage
Kansa
Oto
Missouri
Arapaho
Omaha
Ponca
Arikara
Mandan
Hidatsa
Iowa
Sauk
Fox
Yankton Sioux
Teton Sioux
Kiowa
Cheyenne
Assiniboine
Cree
Shoshone
Salish
Nez Perce
Wishram-Wasco
Chehalis
Wahkiakum
Tillamook
Umatilla
Yakama
Wanapam
Walula
Watlala
Clatsop
Blackfeet
Chinook
Cathlamets
Atsina
Kutenai

</td></tr>
</table>

## Holding a council

Each time the expedition met an Indian nation, they held a "council," or meeting.

First, the expedition's soldiers did drills to show off their training, uniforms, and weapons.

Then a captain made a speech. He said the United States now owned this country, and wanted to be friends. U.S. traders wanted to come here. The Indians should trade with them and not with traders from other countries. The U.S. wanted to help make peace among all Indian nations who were fighting with each other.

**VISITORS PARKING**

*One of the captains (in curved hat) speaks during a council.*

After this speech, the Native American chiefs had their turn to talk. They replied politely, and welcomed the visitors. Sometimes they talked about problems with Indian enemies. They said they hoped for good trading with the U.S. The captains spoke in English. Another man in the Corps would translate this into the language spoken by the tribe.

After smoking a pipe of peace together, each group gave presents to the other.

Finally, the Corps of Discovery demonstrated inventions such as their "spyglass" (small telescope), a compass, and a magnet. Lewis's air gun was a big success. After it was pumped up, the amazing gun fired without gunpowder.

## Mandan and Hidatsa

These people were friendly and informative hosts during the winter of 1804-1805. See page 42.

*The captains called their small telescope a "spyglass."*

# Clark's questions

Dr. Benjamin Rush of Philadelphia gave Lewis a list of questions to ask each Indian nation. Clark was in charge of asking, and was faithful in writing down the answers.

He also asked about other Indian people who lived too far away to be visited. Some things he asked were:

How many people are in your tribe? How many homes? How many warriors? Do you trade with other Indians, and for what? Do you trade with whites? What countries or companies do they come from? Where would you like a trading post built? What do you sell and what do you buy? Do you farm? If so, what do you grow? What nations are your friends and your enemies?

Clark also asked questions about customs and spiritual beliefs.

## Yankton, Teton Sioux

The Sioux on the lower Missouri were familiar with white traders. They assumed the Corps' boats were full of goods so they could trade.

The Yankton Sioux were met at the end of August 1805. They held a friendly council, and said they hoped traders would follow soon. It helped that a French trader married to a Yankton woman was there to translate.

Upriver, in late September, the Teton Sioux were not so friendly. They wanted more gifts and better trade goods. Young warriors once grabbed boat ropes to stop the Corps from leaving. Everyone was on edge, and weapons were drawn on both sides more than once. No one in either group could translate English directly into Sioux, making things difficult.

Still, after three days, the Corps was allowed to leave unharmed.

*Mandan Indians in ornamental dress*

*Fort Leavenworth in Kansas, seen here, was founded only 21 years after the Corps passed this spot heading home in 1806.*

KEEP OFF GRASS

## Metal items

Metal items were popular with Indian hosts because they could not make such things. The Corps started out with dozens of:

**needles**
(sewing and knitting)

**thimbles**

**fish hooks**

**files**

**small bells**

**knives**
(from small to "butcher" size)

**straight-edge razors**

**awls**
(for punching holes in leather)

**tomahawks**

**combs**

**scissors**

**"looking glasses"**
(mirrors of polished pewter)

**"burning glasses"**
(lenses for starting fires)

# Shoshones

The Corps of Discovery first met Shoshones (*show-SHOW-neze*) at Fort Mandan. They were captives far from their home. One of them was Sacagawea. The captains learned that her people hunted near the Missouri's headwaters late in summer. They hunted buffalo on the plains, then went back to their home in the mountains to be safe from enemies.

The Shoshones became very important in the captains' plans. They hoped to buy horses from the Shoshones, and hire them as guides and packers over the Rockies.

As the Corps came closer and closer to the Three Forks, the Missouri's headwaters, they watched sharply for Shoshones. The captains didn't want to scare away Shoshones who might think their hunting guns were an enemy war party.

The Corps sighted Shoshones several times before the people came close enough to talk. Lewis and a small group were the first to meet them. He learned from their chief, Cameahwait, that the Shoshones were afraid Lewis and his men were friends of their enemies.

When Lewis asked him to come back and meet "my brother chief" and a woman "of your nation" at another place, Cameahwait thought it was a trap. He finally agreed to go with Lewis, but he had an idea. Lewis and his men had to trade clothing with some of the Shoshones. If the whites refused, Cameahwait knew better than to go. But white men and Indians exchanged clothing, and they all set off.

When the two groups first saw each other, Sacagawea recognized Shoshone clothing. She signed to Clark that these were her people, and "danced for the joyful sight," he wrote.

Then they made an amazing discovery. Sacagawea was Chief Cameahwait's sister! Their reunion "was really affecting," Lewis wrote. The young woman also met a friend who had been captured with her, but had escaped.

The joined party made a camp in Montana that the captains named "Camp Fortunate." They were very glad to have found the Shoshones, and to have their agreement to help.

*The Missouri River today at Chamberlain, South Dakota. In 1954, Ft. Randall Dam many miles downstream widened the river into Lake Francis Case. This is very different from what the expedition saw here.*

# Salish

Salish people were buffalo hunters and great horse riders. The Blackfeet, their enemies, had pushed them back into the mountains. They went out onto the plains east of the mountains to hunt buffalo, trying to avoid Blackfeet warriors. Sometimes they hunted buffalo with their friends, the Shoshones.

Salish people still tell of how Chief Three Eagles, on the watch for enemies, discovered the Corps of Discovery. This was in September 1805, in a big western Montana valley called Ross's Hole.

Three Eagles saw two leaders riding horses, and men walking behind leading their horses. One man seemed to be painted black for war, but the whole group was too relaxed to be a war party. They dressed in an odd way, not wrapped in blankets. Three Eagles decided this was not an enemy party, and approached.

*In 1912, Charles M. Russell painted this large mural that is in Montana's capitol. It imagines the Salish greeting the Corps.*

Clark wrote that about 400 Salish "received us friendly." To talk with each other, messages "had to pass through several languages before it got in to theirs…"

Still, the two groups camped together and spent a pleasant evening. The Corps stayed until noon the next day. It was the first time the Salish ever met whites.

The Corps bought some of the Salish people's "elegant" horses, as Clark called them. They also traded some goods and tired horses for fresh animals.

# Clatsops

The Corps of Discovery had a peaceful but not extra-friendly relationship with their neighbors around the winter camp of 1805-1806. There were many misunderstandings because none of the Corps was able to speak to the Clatsops in their language.

The Clatsops were used to trading with Europeans who arrived in ships on the Pacific Ocean, and getting what Lewis and Clark called "high prices" in trade goods for food and furs. To the Clatsops, the Corps must have seemed very poor—or just stingy. For example, by mid-January 1806, the Corps had only 120 feet left of large blue beads on strings. They had more white beads, and plenty of red, but the Clatsops thought blue ones were the best. When a Clatsop man visited wearing a garment made of three otter skins, the captains tried to trade. The man would take only blue beads in trade, and his price was 200 feet of them. And the captains just didn't have that many. By winter's end, they even cut brass buttons off their own dress uniforms to trade.

*Trade beads were given to Indians as gifts, or traded for food and other things. These large beads were more than a quarter inch wide.*

The Corps was able to trade for dried fish, wapato roots, furs, basket hats, and even canoes. The captains noted that a canoe was second in value to a man's wife.

Over the winter, game became scarce and the hunters had to go farther from camp to find elk. What they couldn't carry back to the camp, they cached until they could return and get it. Six elk were stolen before men got back for them, and the Clatsops were blamed. When the Corps was leaving for home in March 1806, they needed one more canoe, in the design that worked well in the Columbia estuary's waves. When one of the interpreters suggested just taking a canoe—and considering it payment for the elk—the captains agreed. This was the only time the captains allowed taking something from Native Americans that was not a gift or a trade.

## Nez Perce

The Corps of Discovery first met the Nez Perce people at Weippe (WEE-ipe) Prairie, Idaho, in September 1805. The men, woman, and baby of the Corps had just crossed the Rockies, having to kill horses to eat, and melt snow to drink. The Nez Perce welcomed these strangers with a feast of fish, bison, cooked camas roots and dried berries.

Now the Corps needed to switch back to canoes for going down the Clearwater River, then the Snake, to the Columbia. They knew how to build canoes, and the Nez Perce described the land ahead of them. But the Corps would need the horses again next spring, to cross the Rockies on the homeward trip.

The captains held their usual council meeting. They asked chiefs Twisted Hair and Tetoharsky to care for the horses during the coming winter. They agreed, and did just that. In the spring, when the Corps returned to Nez Perce country, the people had their horses waiting for them.

When the Corps left Weippe Prairie that fall of 1805, the two chiefs even went along part of the way. They traveled ahead of the group to tell their allies that the Corps came in peace. They also served as interpreters with nations living along the Columbia, because they knew languages used as far as The Dalles, Oregon.

## Walula

The Corps had such a pleasant meeting with the Walula, or Walla Walla, Indians in October 1805 that their chief, Yelleppit, invited them to stay longer.

The Walula were on the Columbia River south of Kennewick, Washington. Chief Yelleppit gave the captains a basket of "mashed berries" and all camped together. Private Pierre Cruzatte played his fiddle in the evening, which the Walula enjoyed.

The captains told Yelleppit that next year, when they returned, they would stay and visit with his people longer.

The next April near the mouth of the Walla Walla River, the Corps stopped with the Walulas for four nights. Wood was scarce in this country, and dried shrubs were burned for fuel. Chief Yelleppit urged his people to share fuel and food with the Corps. Then he set the example by delivering an armload of fuel and a platter of roasted fish.

During the visit, a dance was held until late one night. The captains treated some medical problems among the Walula and their neighbors, the Yakima.

Chief Yelleppit brought Captain Clark a fine white horse, and wanted to trade it for a kettle. By now, the Corps had only enough kettles left for their own cooking. Yelleppit said he'd trade for whatever Clark thought "proper." The captain noticed Yelleppit admiring his own officer's sword, and traded that.

On the third day, the village lent canoes and helped the Corps take their horses and baggage across the Columbia. But Yelleppit, the host, required one thing in return: the Corps must stay another night.

When it turned out that the Walula had a Shoshone captive living among them, Sacagawea interpreted through her, and so communication here was very good.

Chief Yelleppit gave the captains the biggest gift of all when he described a shortcut to take across the southeast corner of Washington. Instead of going upriver on the Snake (the way they had come), they could go on land past today's Waitsburg to meet the Clearwater River.

When the Corps took their leave of "these friendly honest people," Clark rode the "elegant" white horse.

*A Nez Perce elder on his horse, late in the 1800s.*

*Peace pipe*

# Blackfeet

A few members of the Corps met some Piegan (*pee*-GAN) Blackfeet on the homeward trip in 1806. This council ended with a fight between the Corps and Native Americans. It was the only time the Corps fired upon and killed Indians.

On the trip west, the Corps had reached the mouth of the Marias River in Montana, in June 1805. Most of the men thought the wide river was actually the Missouri. It was worth exploring, but they didn't have time.

Now, in July 1806, Captain Lewis took privates Joseph and Reubin Field, and interpreter George Drouillard, up the Marias River. They knew they were in the Blackfeet's land. Other tribes, enemies of the Blackfeet, had described the Blackfeet as warlike and dangerous.

When Lewis's small group met eight Blackfeet men on the Two Medicine River, he was tense. Still, he got off his horse and walked toward them to show he was friendly.

The twelve sat down for a council, and Lewis gave three chiefs each a peace medal, an American flag, and a handkerchief. They smoked the pipe and talked in sign language.

Lewis urged the Blackfeet to make peace with their enemies. He tried to say that the captains had made peace treaties between other warring tribes they met. He tried to say also that the U.S. would trade with peaceful nations.

The Blackfeet thought he said that the captains had gathered all their enemies together and would give them guns. This was a serious threat.

Still, the two groups camped together that night. Men of the Corps took turns standing watch.

At dawn, one of the chiefs grabbed the Field brothers' rifles. Two others took Lewis's and Drouillard's guns. In getting the rifles back, Reubin Field stabbed the chief and killed him. He still wore the peace medal given to him the day before.

Lewis drew his pistol on the man who had taken his rifle. When that warrior dropped the rifle, Lewis didn't shoot and wouldn't let his other men shoot him.

Then the Blackfeet tried to drive off the Corps' horses, so they'd be stranded on the prairie. The Corps chased them, and Lewis shot one warrior who fell but shot back. Lewis felt the bullet whiz by his head.

The Blackfeet rode off, and the four men of the Corps returned to the campsite. Lewis took back the flag, but left the peace medal around the dead chief's neck so the Blackfeet would know who had killed the man.

During the council, Lewis had told the Blackfeet that another group of his men was waiting at the mouth of the Marias River. He invited them to get more of their people and go there for a council. Now, his tiny group needed to hurry to the Marias to warn the 19 men camped there before the Blackfeet war party arrived.

Quickly mounting their horses, Lewis, the Field brothers, and Drouillard galloped off, and rode until three o'clock that afternoon. After resting, they rode on until two in the morning, covering 100 miles. They slept a few hours and got up at dawn. They were "so sore" that they "could scarcely stand," Lewis wrote.

Amazingly, when they reached the Missouri River west of the Marias, here came their men in canoes, headed for the mouth of the Marias. Lewis and his three men let the horses go. They quickly dug up caches and continued downriver in the canoes.

*Trade goods like these were used as gifts and money by the Corps. Mirrors are at the bottom right, fire-starting lens at left.*

*Blackfeet Indians at Montana's Sweetgrass Hills*

# What they learned...

## Many creatures and plants

the Expedition learned about were related to animals already known to science. Some were completely new to science. And some were known in Europe but had not been seen in North America before.

Indians described some of these animals and plants before Lewis and Clark saw them. The captains asked what uses Native Americans made of the plants, and asked how the animals lived. Some plants, such as yampah (which tastes like anise), Sacagawea gathered and cooked.

Mountain goats live high up on rocky mountaintops. The Shoshones showed the Corps some skins of this animal, but Lewis and Clark never got close to a living one.

## Bison

The American bison (often called buffalo) had once lived as far east as New York.

By 1804, bison had been forced out of the East. But vast herds still roamed the Great Plains. Maybe 60 million animals lived there. Most members of the Corps of Discovery had never seen a bison. They saw their first herd at the mouth of the Kansas River in Kansas.

At the Great Falls of the Missouri in 1805, Lewis wrote: "I sincerely believe that there were not less than 10,000 buffalo within a circle of 2 miles around that place..."

On the Yellowstone River in August 1805, Clark's group had to stop for an hour while a "gang of buffalo," as he wrote, crossed the river. He said the river near the eastern edge of Montana was a mile wide at this point. The bison stretched across the whole distance. Later in the day they saw two more "gangs" just as large.

## Grizzly bears

Before leaving Camp Dubois, the men heard about a very large, fierce bear. It lived on the upper Missouri. Its hair was light at the ends, giving it a grayish, silvery, or whitish look. Lewis often called it the "white bear," and some people still call it the "silver-tip." "Grizzle" is an old word for gray hair. Grizzly bears come in shades from dark brown to blond.

When Lewis heard Indians talk about the grizzly, he thought their fear was because they had only bows and arrows to fight it. With guns, he wrote, "skilled riflemen" would have no trouble.

But after the Corps met a few grizzlies, Lewis saw they were just as fierce whether facing guns or bows.

## Caches

The French boatmen taught the army men how to make a cache (pronounced *cash*). Lewis called it a small "cellar." Both Indians and whites used this method to store possessions and even food. They dug a pit in the ground and lined it with grass, sticks, and hides. After putting inside what they wanted to store, they covered it over with the same materials, plus dirt.

The Corps made important caches near the Great Falls, leaving supplies for the homeward trip. Lewis also cached plant specimens in one. Unfortunately, spring flood water got into that one and ruined the preserved plants.

On the return trip, the Corps stopped at the Great Falls to pick up the white pirogue and five canoes. The red pirogue at mouth of Marias was too decayed to take, so they took its hardware.

*Lewis and Clark called prairie dogs "barking squirrels."*

## Mammals

badger
plains grizzly bear
black–tailed prairie dog
mountain beaver
Audubon bighorn sheep
(now extinct)
mule deer
(which Lewis named for its long ears)
thirteen–lined ground squirrel
Oregon bobcat
coyote
gray wolf
pack rat
(bushy–tailed woodrat)
swift fox
white–tailed jackrabbit
wolverine
mountain goat
harbor seal
Columbian black–tailed deer

## Pemmican

For Plains Indians, pemmican was a convenient food when traveling. After jerking (drying) meat, women pounded it into powder. Then they mixed hot fat—and berries, if available—into the meat. This mixture was dried into cakes. It kept a long time, was a high-energy "fast" food, and could be carried anywhere.

The Corps first learned of it from the Teton Sioux, who served it along with boiled dog meat at a banquet. In 1805 and 1806, the journal-writers mention making pemmican of their own. At Fort Clatsop before the homeward trip, they may have used dried fish, with whale blubber as the fat.

*Making pemmican by pounding meat, fat, and berries together.*

*After the expedition passed Pelican Island, their boats were caught several times by sandbars. Dams built during the 20th century have made the Missouri River deeper in this area today.*

*"Jerking" or drying meat.*

## Pelicans by the thousands

Near Little Sioux, Iowa, in August 1804, Lewis wrote: "I saw a great number of feathers floating down the river...[covering] sixty or seventy yards of the breadth of the river. For three miles..., we did not perceive from whence they came...[Then] we were surprised by the appearance of a flock of pelican at rest on a large sand bar...; they appeared to cover several acres of ground."

XING

## Carolina parakeet

*These birds have been extinct since the 1920's, killed off by farmers.*

## Lewis's woodpecker

*Captain Lewis first noted this lively small bird on July 20, 1805, in a shadowy canyon near Helena, Montana, as "a black woodpecker…as black as a crow." He killed some as specimens the following May 27, in Idaho, and wrote about them in detail including the crimson face and other colors. The skin of one of these birds is in a museum at Harvard University, and is the only animal specimen left from the expedition, as far as historians know.*

## Clark's nutcracker

*In Idaho, exploring the Salmon River on August 22, 1805, Captain Clark first wrote about a bird the size of a robin, which he saw cracking open pine cones to eat the nuts inside. It had been unknown to scientists. Later, an ornithologist (scientist who studies birds) named this type of bird for Clark.*

# Mosquitoes and gnats and animal fat

Along the rivers, mosquitoes were a horrible problem. Everyone was covered with bites, and some bites became infected.

On the homeward trip, Clark wrote that Pompy's little face was "much puffed & swelled" from mosquito bites. Sometimes, Seaman, the dog, howled with pain from bites under his thick hair. The people probably wanted to howl, too.

Thick swarms of gnats were another problem. Everyone got gnats in their eyes, noses, and mouths!

The only thing the people could do was smear their skin with bear or bison fat. It seemed to help a little.

## Birds

Carolina parakeet
(now extinct)
Oregon ruffed grouse
white-fronted goose
California condor
sage grouse
least tern
black-billed magpie
willet
Lewis's woodpecker
western meadowlark
blue grouse
pinyon jay
McCown's longspur
Steller's jay
sharp-tailed grouse
gray jay
spruce grouse
Clark's nutcracker

## Fish

steelhead trout
westslope cutthroat trout
sauger
candlefish
goldeneye
mountain sucker

## Reptiles

bullsnake
prairie rattlesnake
soft-shelled turtle

On Montana's Yellowstone River in July 1806, Clark wrote that if he tried to estimate the number of types of animals along its valley, it would be incredible. "I shall therefore be silent on the subject," he wrote.

## Prickly pear cactus

Captain Lewis had had an amazing day in Montana on July 14, 1805. First, he found five waterfalls on the Missouri River where he had expected only one. Then, he survived an encounter with a grizzly bear when his gun was empty. As he was headed back to his small advance party in the dark, Lewis thought about his "curious adventures" and how it almost seemed like he was under a magic spell. "...I thought it might be a dream, but the prickly pears which pierced my feet very severely once in a while, particularly after it grew dark, convinced me that I was really awake..."

The next day he said this low cactus was "one of the beauties as well as the greatest pests of the plains."

Several weeks later, near Helena, Clark wrote that his feet were "constantly stuck full [of] prickly pear thorns, I pulled out 17 by the light of the fire..."

Even after crossing the Rockies, they found prickly pear along the upper Columbia. On October 17, near Richland, Washington, Clark wrote that the prickly pear there was worse "than I have before seen."

All the men sewed extra soles on their moccasins, but the cactus still poked through.

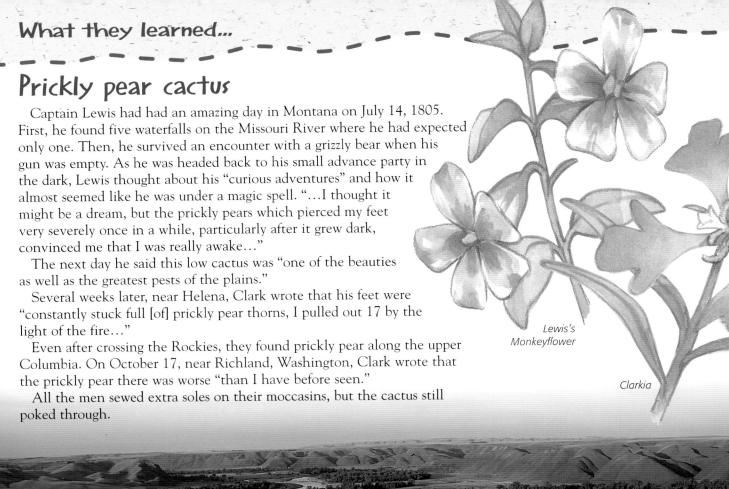

Lewis's
Monkeyflower

Clarkia

**Prickly pear cactus along
the Marias River in Montana**

# Roots to eat

Men of the Corps of Discovery were used to eating root vegetables such as potatoes, turnips, and onions. In 1805 and 1806, they learned from Indian people how to prepare roots that grew along their path. Some became important parts of their diet.

**Breadroot**—Sacagawea introduced the men to this near the Milk River in Montana, May 1805. It was eaten raw when fresh, and dried over fires to save. Whole dried breadroot was boiled with meat. Powdered dried breadroot was used to thicken soup or make a "pudding" with berries and buffalo marrow.

**Bitterroot**—The Shoshones carried along dried bitterroot and shared it with Lewis in southwestern Montana, August 1805. He boiled it as they told him, but didn't like the bitter taste. They ate his portion "heartily."

**Camas** (*CAM-uhs*)—First encountered by Clark at Weippe Prairie, Idaho, in September 1805, served by Nez Perce he met. Several tribes came here to harvest and dry camas every summer. He enjoyed the bread made from it, and also ate some of the roots.

**Cous** (*rhymes with goose*)—The Corps first saw this at the Cascades of the Columbia, near Beacon Rock. On their homeward trip in 1806, they often bought it from Native Americans along the Columbia. Cous was ready to be gathered earlier in spring than camas. The root was skinned and pounded into thick disks, then sun-dried. The disks were eaten as "bread" or boiled to make thick broth. Lewis liked the broth version better.

**Wapato** (*WOPP-uh-toe*)—Watlala Indians on the Columbia introduced this water plant. Its roots were harvested by women wading in ponds where it grew. They pulled the roots up with their feet and put them into small canoes. Several tribes gathered it and traded with others nearer the Pacific coast. The Corps depended on wapato, used like potato, during their winter at Fort Clatsop.

**Yampah** (*YAMP-uh*)—Sacagawea gathered some in Idaho on the homeward trip. This root has an anise taste.

# Pacific Ocean traders

Americans knew that ships from other nations traded along the Pacific coast. President Jefferson and Lewis had thought that maybe some men could come home with them. In those days, ships had to travel around the southern tip of South America. It was a long trip. Going home that way was no faster or safer than returning on foot and by canoe.

By the time the captains reached the Pacific, though, they had decided against that plan. By now they thought their group shouldn't be too small in case of trouble.

Captain Clark questioned Indians around Fort Clatsop about the traders. He had trouble understanding their answers. It seemed the ships arrived in the spring and fall. The same traders came year after year. Clark knew that they couldn't be coming all the way from Great Britain. The voyage took too long by sailing ship to make a round trip in one year.

Clark thought that the traders must use island bases somewhere far out in the Pacific. He was right. European ships carried goods to islands like Hawaii, where other ships picked them up to take to Europe. Other traders also bought these goods with what they'd purchased in China, such as fine silks. Then they took the new supply of European goods and traded with north Pacific coast Indians for furs. They took the furs to China and traded before returning to their South Pacific island base.

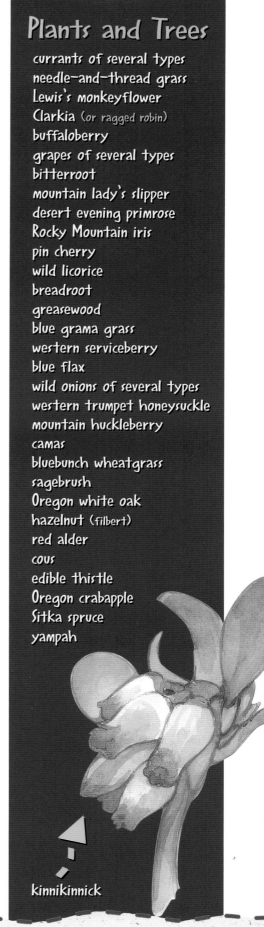

## Plants and Trees

- currants of several types
- needle-and-thread grass
- Lewis's monkeyflower
- Clarkia (or ragged robin)
- buffaloberry
- grapes of several types
- bitterroot
- mountain lady's slipper
- desert evening primrose
- Rocky Mountain iris
- pin cherry
- wild licorice
- breadroot
- greasewood
- blue grama grass
- western serviceberry
- blue flax
- wild onions of several types
- western trumpet honeysuckle
- mountain huckleberry
- camas
- bluebunch wheatgrass
- sagebrush
- Oregon white oak
- hazelnut (filbert)
- red alder
- cous
- edible thistle
- Oregon crabapple
- Sitka spruce
- yampah

kinnikinnick

# What they ate...

Food rations were given out on this schedule: On the first day, dried corn and grease, the next day salt pork and flour, and the third day cornmeal and pork. Then the cycle repeated.

The pork was salted to preserve it.

When the men were successful hunting or fishing, fresh meat replaced the salt pork.

The evening meal was called "supper." When they set up camp for the night, they cooked enough food for that meal and for the next day. That way, when they stopped for "dinner," their mid-day meal, the Corps ate leftovers and didn't have to build a fire.

In the morning, they started off at sunrise, then stopped for a breakfast of leftovers around eight o'clock.

The men soon became lazy about cooking their meals and cleaning up afterward. The captains assigned a cook for each squad, who had to prepare food soon after it was received, and take care of the kitchen utensils. In return, those three men no longer had to help pitch tents or search for firewood.

**The Corps of Discovery** could not carry along enough food for the whole trip. Lewis purchased enough army rations for 4,200 meals, which sounds like a very large amount. That would last 1,400 days for only one person. But 30 people would run out of meals after lunch on the 47th day!

They had to fish and hunt along the way, and buy food (using trade goods) from Indians. Sometimes, while traveling, they could gather fresh vegetables or fruits.

But their diet was mostly meat. They needed its protein and fat for the constant hard work they were doing. But filling up on meat all the time was not a good diet.

## How to eat flour

The Corps set out with more than 5,500 servings of flour in 21 big barrels and some smaller kegs. They left some in the cache at the Great Falls in July 1805, to use on the return trip the next year.

They used flour to thicken meat stews, and also made dumplings—balls of soft dough dropped into hot stew to cook.

In August, Lewis's advance party was just about out of flour when they met the Shoshones. With his next-to-last pound, Lewis made a "pudding" by cooking flour, water, and berries. Chief Cameahwait said it was the best thing he had eaten in a while. For the last pound of flour, Lewis had no more berries, and simply stirred flour into boiling water—and served it to six people. Clark's advance group ran out of flour the next month, but then in November Sacagawea surprised the whole Corps by making a bread from some flour she had been saving. Even though it had gotten wet and "sour," Clark said the bread was welcome.

*Trenchers, like this reproduction, were sturdy wooden dinner plates used in frontier homes and supplied to army men. There's a well for salt, and the center can work as a bowl.*

## Dogs and horses

Some Indian people served dog meat to the Corps as a special treat, and others ate this meat regularly. Some Corps members liked the meat. Lewis, who brought a pet dog along for the trip, enjoyed eating dog meat. But Clark couldn't stand the thought, and would eat a meal of only root vegetables rather than touch dog.

During the Rocky Mountain crossing, there was almost no game in the mountains. It was September, and snow covered the high mountains. When they completely ran out of meat, the men killed a colt to eat. Five days later, after having nothing to eat the night before, they killed a stray horse for food.

## Maple sugar

At Camp Dubois, as spring 1804 neared, maple sap rose in the trees. The men tapped the trees and boiled the syrup to make sugar. Many of them probably had done this at home.

For Sacagawea, sugar was a very unusual treat, and she liked it. She later shared some with her brother, who also had never had it and thought it delicious.

To "jerk," or dry, meat, you cut it into thin slices and hang it up if the air is dry, or above a fire. This is an Indian drying rack from later in the 1800s.

## Fresh salmon versus dried

The Corps reached the Columbia River in autumn 1805 during the fall salmon run. Villages of many different nations were set up along the river, as people dried salmon for the winter.

Lewis and Clark didn't understand that the salmon naturally died after spawning. Gathered right away, these were fresh, healthy salmon. The captains saw fish on the shore and thought they had died from illness. They insisted on eating only dried salmon. They assumed it had been caught the usual way.

## Portable Soup

Lewis bought 193 pounds of "portable soup," an army ration of the day. It was either powdered, or a very thick liquid, and contained some of the same things as instant soup today: powdered or finely chopped vegetables, and meat broth.

# Being sick or hurt...

**No doctor** was on the Lewis and Clark Expedition. In 1803, in Philadelphia, Lewis took lessons from three doctors—for only four weeks. During that time, he was also studying navigation and buying supplies for the trip. The doctors taught Lewis what he needed to know for situations they thought could happen in the wilderness.

**FIRST AID**

On the trip, Lewis usually administered medicine to people of the Corps. He and Clark also treated illnesses among Indian people they met, even setting broken bones and amputating frostbitten toes.

Illnesses and injuries happened often. At the end of July 1805, beyond the Missouri River's headwaters but before meeting the Shoshones and getting horses, Lewis wrote: "We have a lame crew just now, two with...bad boils..., one with a bad stone bruise, one with his arm accidentally dislocated but fortunately well replaced, and a fifth has strained his back by slipping and falling backwards on...[a] canoe."

## Snake and mosquito bites

The men suffered snakebites from time to time. Perhaps the snake was one new to them, so they didn't know if it was poisonous. They had to treat each one as if it were.

The treatment shows that some old herbal remedies became important modern drugs. To draw out the poison, one of the captains would apply a poultice (a wet, warm mixture) made with powdered cinchona (*sin-CONE-uh*). This was a bark that South American Indians had used for centuries to lower fever. Lewis and Clark knew it as "Peruvian bark."

*Prairie rattlesnakes live along the Missouri today, just as they did then.*

Today, cinchona is used in making quinine, a medicine for malaria, which causes chills and fever. At the time of the expedition, no one knew malaria was carried by mosquitoes.

## Icky insect repellent

Mosquitoes and gnats were sometimes so thick that the men smeared their skin with animal fat to keep from getting bitten.

## Treating Pryor's shoulder

Sergeant Nathaniel Pryor had trouble with his shoulder, which often was painfully dislocated. In November 1804, Clark wrote: "Sergeant Pryor... put his shoulder out of place, we made four trials before we replaced it[.]"

One myth of the time was that it was okay to drink lots of cold water on a hot day—if you wet your face, hands and feet first! The men of the Corps were careful to do this.

# The dangerous homeward trip

Some very serious injuries occurred on the trip home in 1806.

• On June 18, in Idaho's Bitterroot range, Private John Potts cut his leg with a large knife. Lewis wrote that, using a tourniquet, he had "much difficulty" stopping the bleeding. The wound became infected and painful. Lewis cured the infection with poultices.

• On July 18, Private George Gibson was in Clark's group going down the Yellowstone River. He had shot a deer. When he tried to get back on his horse, it bucked and he fell on a branch that was one inch thick. It was pushed two inches into his leg. Captain Clark, who never wasted words, wrote: "This is a very bad wound and pains him exceedingly. I dressed the wound."

By morning, Gibson's leg hurt from knee to hip. He couldn't sit in a saddle. Clark had the "strongest and gentlest" horse saddled, then the group piled skins and blankets on its saddle. Gibson could lie back, but in a couple hours his pain was too much to ride.

Clark now wanted to make a canoe for Gibson. Trees in this area were very small. So the men made two small canoes and tied them together.

Thirteen days later, Clark wrote that Gibson could walk now, and had gone out from camp and shot an antelope.

• On August 11, Captain Lewis was shot by Cruzatte when the two were hunting elk near the Missouri. The bullet went through Lewis's left thigh and grazed the back of his right one.

Thinking it was an Indian attack, Lewis ran "100 paces" toward the river and called to the men on shore. They ran to him, and Lewis sent them to rescue Cruzatte from the imagined Indians. With difficulty, Lewis made his way back to a boat and prepared all his weapons.

The rescue party returned with Cruzatte, and reported no sign of Indians.

Lewis soon figured out that Cruzatte had shot him accidentally. In the willows where they'd been hunting, Lewis's brown leather clothing must have looked like an elk to the one-eyed fiddler. Cruzatte was just as sure he hadn't shot Lewis, but rather an elk that had gotten away.

Lewis had to dress his own wounds. The men canoed downstream for two days, and met the rest of the Corps. Lewis applied a poultice of cinchona to his wounds and lay on his belly for 11 days. His wounds eventually healed.

*Lolo Hot Springs, Montana. The Corps stopped here twice to soak in the springs, just as local Indians did.*

## Sergeant Charles Floyd

Despite all the injuries and accidents the Corps had, Sergeant Floyd was the only man who died on the trip. He died in August 1804 of infection caused by a ruptured appendix.

At the time, no doctor in the world knew how to treat this illness. Today, surgery to remove an unhealthy appendix is common.

Floyd died where Sergeant Bluff, Iowa, later was built. The Corps gave him a military funeral on a high bluff now a mile from the Missouri River. The original burial site is still called Sergeant Bluff.

On the homeward trip, the Corps stopped to pay their respects. They found the grave had been dug open, and refilled it. The cedar grave marker they had placed in 1804 was a landmark on the river until 1857.

Because of river floods, and railroad construction in the area, Sergeant Floyd's bones were moved in 1857 to a safer site in Sioux City. In 1901, an obelisk (a small tower shaped like the Washington Monument) was built at this grave.

# When it was winter...

REST AREA NEXT RIGHT

## Camp Dubois: the first winter

The captains said their expedition officially began when they left this place on May 14, 1804. But by that time the Corps' army members already had spent five months together.

They built this "camp" in December 1803 on land across both the Missouri and the Mississippi rivers from St. Louis. That city was then a frontier town of only 1,000 to 1,400 people. Today the camp's site is in Illinois, because the Mississippi River has shifted.

Captain Clark managed the camp, while Lewis often was away making arrangements for the trip—right up to the last minute. Clark wrote notes on who was a good soldier, and what special skills the men had, from being a good hunter or runner to knowing carpentry or metalworking. These notes helped the captains decide whom to choose for the permanent party, the one that went to the Pacific Ocean.

**During winter,** the Corps could not travel. Rivers were frozen, snow was deep, and game was scarce. They had to stop and stay in shelters. They stayed at Camp Dubois (winter 1803-1804) in Illinois, Fort Mandan (winter 1804-1805) in North Dakota, and Fort Clatsop (winter 1805-1806) in Oregon.

Fort Mandan and Fort Clatsop sound like big, permanent places, but they were not. They were leaky, cramped little wooden buildings inside tall fences, which the Corps had to build for themselves. None of the winter sites was a true fort.

## Fort Mandan: the planning winter

The Mandan-Hidatsa (MANN-*dann*)/(*hid-AHT-suh*) villages in North Dakota were a large and important trading center on the Missouri River. The captains thought the five villages held about 4,400 people—three or four times the number in St. Louis then!

The Mandan raised hardy crops in this land of below-zero winters and blazing hot summers. Their corn, squash, beans, and sunflower seeds attracted Indians and whites who came to trade for them. The Hidatsa hunted buffalo and other game on the plains. They sold furs to British traders who made a nine-day journey from a post in Canada.

A tall fence surrounded each village. The people lived in domed lodges made of earth, a good way to keep out the cold. Later, white homesteaders in the area made homes using wide "bricks" of cut sod.

The Corps built their winter home of wood, though. It was small, and in the shape of a triangle. Huts made up two sides, and a fence with a gate stretched across the third side. They named it in honor of their neighbors, who visited almost every day.

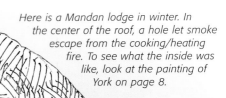

*Here is a Mandan lodge in winter. In the center of the roof, a hole let smoke escape from the cooking/heating fire. To see what the inside was like, look at the painting of York on page 8.*

# Fort Clatsop: the last winter

This cramped wooden "fort" was chilly, damp, and filled with fleas that loved the rainy climate. The Corps were hungry most of the time. When the hunters found elk, others tried to dry some for jerky to eat on the trip home. But in the dampness, the meat spoiled even while hanging over fires kept going all the time.

*Fort Clatsop reconstruction today (near Astoria, Oregon) is based on a floor plan that Clark drew.*

The sun came out on only six days out of 141 at Fort Clatsop. Only 12 days were without rain.

The Corps didn't find many friends among their neighbors, and visitors didn't arrive as they had at Fort Mandan. Also, the most exciting part of the trip was over. What they faced was mostly going back the way they came. They were anxious to be home. They knew from the Nez Perce that they'd have to wait to cross the Rockies because of deep snow. Even so, they left Fort Clatsop earlier than they should have. Just to be going home.

One neighbor the captains liked was Clatsop Chief Coboway, the "most friendly and decent" person in the area, Lewis wrote. When the Corps headed home, they gave him Fort Clatsop. He lived there for some years. In 1899, one of his grandsons pointed out the fort's exact site to a researcher.

*In January and February 1806, three men at a time stayed at a camp near the Pacific, 15 miles away from Fort Clatsop, at Seaside, Oregon. It was called the Salt Works. Pictured here is the memorial at Seaside that imagines what the "salt factory" might have looked like.*
*The men's job was to keep kettles of ocean water boiling, and save the salt left after the water evaporated. The Corps would use the salt in their food on the return trip, and also trade it to Indians along the way.*

## Quizzing visitors

What the captains learned during the winter at Fort Mandan was very important for planning the rest of their trip. They quizzed every Indian and white visitor about what was ahead. Maps and writings from other explorers could not tell them about the land between here and the far end of the Columbia River.

Not all the information they heard was correct. For example, people they talked to didn't make it clear that the Rockies held many ranges of mountains. But they made the captains understand that they'd need horses to cross.

People told the captains that the Shoshones lived where they'd cross the Rockies. These people could supply the horses and show them a trail to use.

Needing to trade with Shoshones, whose language no Corps member spoke, was a new problem. But the solution was right here in the villages.

A French-Canadian the captains met here had a Shoshone wife. The captains hired Toussaint Charbonneau and Sacagawea as interpreters.

Something else the captains learned shaped their plans for 1805, the year ahead. The Rockies were high, and winter snows came early. They would need to cross in early fall. But they couldn't leave the villages in the spring until ice broke up on the Missouri, in early April. No one could tell them how many miles they had to travel to the Rockies.

# To relax or celebrate...

**FUN AHEAD**

## Christmases from best to poor

At Camp Dubois, Captain Clark wrote: "I was wakened by a Christmas discharge [of guns]...the men frolicked and hunted all day,... several turkey killed. Shields returned with a cheese and 4 lb. butter..."

At Fort Mandan, Sergeant Ordway wrote: "We had the best to eat that could be had, & continued firing [guns], dancing & frolicking during the whole day."

At Fort Clatsop, Captain Clark wrote: "Our dinner today consisted of poor elk boiled, spoiled fish & some roots, a bad Christmas dinner."

It was a Southern custom to fire guns in celebration. Christmas and New Year's mornings began with a volley of shots in the Corps' winter forts, followed by shouts and songs.

## The Corps of Discovery's work

was exhausting and dangerous. Still, they sometimes played. In the evenings, they might sing songs or listen to fiddle music. They also used music to entertain Indians they visited, and enjoyed the Indians' music. They celebrated holidays as well as they could, even when food and presents were scarce.

## Fourth of July

In 1804, on the Missouri River near Atchison, Kansas, Sergeant Floyd wrote: "We fired our bow piece [the keelboat's small cannon] this morning and & one in the evening for Independence of the U.S."

In 1805, the men spent the day pushing wagons on the portage around the Great Falls. Lewis wrote: "Our work being at an end this evening...the fiddle was played and [the men] danced very merrily until 9 in the evening when a heavy shower of rain put an end to that part of the amusement tho' they continued their mirth with songs and festive jokes and were extremely merry until late at night."

In 1806, the captains were leading separate groups in Montana. Clark, along the Bitterroot River, wrote: "This being the day of the declaration of independence of the United States and a day commonly celebrated by my country, I had every disposition to celebrate this day..." He called an early halt for dinner (the mid-day meal) and the party "partook of a sumptuous dinner" of roast venison and cous mush. Lewis's journal on that Fourth of July doesn't mention the holiday.

*Replica of the 15-star American flag of which the expedition carried an unknown number, in three sizes*

*Musical instruments on the trip were a violin (usually called a "fiddle" by the men), a jaw harp (which makes a rhythmic twanging and plays more than one note), and a tambourine.*

DANCE NEXT EXIT

# Come to the dance!

Many times, the men danced by themselves and for or with Indians they met.

In eastern Washington, in 1806, they visited the Walula Indians. These people invited nearby Yakima Indians to join them. Clark thought about 550 Native Americans were there.

In the evening, the fiddle was tuned up and members of the Corps danced for about an hour. Then the Indians danced. When some men of the Corps joined the Indians in dancing, their hosts were delighted. The fun continued until 10 p.m.

*When the Corps met the Teton Sioux in future South Dakota, the warriors had just returned from a raid, and performed a scalp dance. Of course, there were no cameras. These Sioux dancers are pictured in the Black Hills.*

**In Montana on the homeward trip,** the Corps of Discovery split into five groups. Each had a different job and different direction to go. They began to divide at Traveler's Rest, their camp near Lolo in western Montana. They planned to meet each other at the mouth of the Yellowstone River, in North Dakota.

## Exploring the Marias and the Yellowstone

First, Captain Lewis took nine men and left the bigger group. Five Nez Perce men went part-way to point out their shortcut to the Great Falls.

At the falls, Lewis left Sergeant Gass and privates Thompson, Goodrich, McNeal, Werner, Frazer. They would start opening the Upper Portage cache and wait for men bringing canoes down the Missouri.

Lewis, with the Field brothers and interpreter Drouillard, went overland to the Marias River. This was the one most of the men had thought was the true Missouri when they passed it the year before.

Captain Clark and all the others went from Traveler's Rest to the Three Forks. There, Sergeant Ordway took nine men down the Missouri in canoes left last fall. Along with Gass and his five men, they portaged canoes and the remaining supplies back around the Great Falls. This took 11 days.

Then they floated down the river, planning to wait for Lewis at the mouth of the Marias.

At the Three Forks with Clark's group, Sacagawea said she remembered the way the Shoshones traveled to the Yellowstone. She led the men over Bozeman Pass and they came to the river near Livingston.

At the river, a fifth group of Corps members split off. Sergeant Pryor led privates Hall, Shannon, and Windsor. They were planning to herd most of the horses to the Mandan-Hidatsa villages, then north to a Canadian trading post. But horses were stolen, and Pryor's men had to take to the river. They met Clark's group on the Missouri in North Dakota. The site is now under Garrison Dam.

Mosquitoes and bears sent Clark's new group downriver. Lewis's combined group met them at what's now called Reunion Point, in North Dakota.

*J. K. Ralston painted this picture. It imagines Clark's group when they saw the Yellowstone River ahead, on July 15, 1806.*

*Yellowstone River near Livingston, Montana, where Captain Clark's party reached it to explore downstream on their homeward trip.*

## Sacagawea's family

The Charbonneau family left the expedition where they had joined it, at the Mandan-Hidatsa villages in North Dakota. For their service, they were paid $500.33⅓.

Captain Clark asked them to let him take Pompy home with him. Living with Clark, he could go to school in St. Louis. Sacagawea said he was too young, at age two, to leave his mother. When he was four, she said, it would be okay.

## But you're dead!

No one in the U. States—as Lewis and Clark called it—had heard from the expedition since the return party reached St. Louis in spring 1805. On the Missouri River near St. Joseph, Missouri and near the Grand River, the Corps met two parties of traders. They learned that the rumor back home said all of them had been killed, or captured by Spaniards and put to work in silver mines in the Southwest. The men stayed up late with the trappers listening to news from home.

CATTLE CROSSING

### Let's hear it for cows!

After all the interesting new animals the men had seen, they were excited to see plain old cows again. This was on September 20, 1806, near St. Charles, Missouri. The men gave a big cheer. They knew they were close to home!

# Exploring...

*Fort Clatsop in Oregon has an area where visitors can try on clothing like the Corps wore.*

## Websites

**www.lewis-clark.org**
is a multi-media site called "Discovering Lewis and Clark"

**www.lewisandclark.com**
offers information, books for sale, and useful links

**www.lewisandclark.org**
is the site of Lewis and Clark Trail Heritage Foundation

## About the author

Barbara Fifer is co-author with Vicky Soderberg of "Along the Trail with Lewis and Clark" (published by Montana Magazine books, 1998), and also wrote "Everyday U.S. Geography" (Doubleday Direct, 2000) and "Along the Trail with Lewis and Clark Travel Planner and Guide" (Montana Magazine, 2000).

## Entire trail

Lewis and Clark National Historic Trail, 1709 Jackson St., Omaha, NE 68102. This National Park Service office works with public and private, state, and local agencies.

Lewis and Clark Trail Heritage Foundation, P.O. Box 3434, Great Falls, MT 59403. An organization for anyone interested in studying the expedition. They publish *We Proceeded On*, a quarterly magazine.

## Idaho
Weippe Prairie/Nez Perce National Historic Park, Weippe

## Illinois
Lewis and Clark State Historic Site, Hartford

## Iowa
Lewis and Clark Monument Park, Council Bluffs
Sergeant Floyd Monument, Sioux City

## Kansas
Frontier Army Museum, Fort Leavenworth

## Missouri
Clark's Point, Kansas City
Jefferson National Expansion Memorial, St. Louis
Missouri Historical Society, St. Louis

## Montana
Lewis and Clark National Trail Interpretive Center, Great Falls
Missouri Headwaters State Park, Three Forks
Pompeys Pillar National Historical Landmark, near Billings

## Nebraska
Fort Atkinson State Historic Park is near where the Corps held their first council with Indians, at town of Fort Calhoun

## North Dakota
Fort Mandan Historic Site, and Lewis and Clark Interpretive Center, Washburn
Knife River Villages National Historic Site, Stanton
North Dakota Heritage Center, Bismarck

## Oregon
Fort Clatsop National Memorial, Astoria
Salt Works, Seaside

## South Dakota
Fort Pierre National Grass Land, Fort Pierre
South Dakota Cultural Heritage Center, Pierre

## Washington
Chief Timothy State Park, Clarkston
Lewis and Clark Interpretive Center, Ilwaco
Sacajawea State Park, Pasco